Why Do Dogs Do That?

By Nancy White • Illustrated by Gioia Fiammenghi

Scholastic Inc.

New York Toronto London Auckland Sydney

Dedication/Acknowledgments

To all the kids at Osborne Manor

Acknowledgment

To Dr. Karen Overall at the School of Veterinary Medicine of the University of Pennsylvania, I offer most sincere thanks for sharing your expertise and fascinating insights into the world of dogs and why they do the things they do. Your suggestions, corrections, and additions to the manuscript worked to the great advantage of this book.

ISBN 0-590-26597-0

Text copyright © 1995 by Nancy White.
Illustrations copyright © 1995 by Gioia Frammenghi
All rights reserved.   Published by Scholastic Inc.

12 11 10 9 8 7 6 5 4 3   6 7 8 9/9 0/0

Printed in the U.S.A.   23

First Scholastic printing, December 1995

Book design by Laurie Williams

Contents

INTRODUCTION

Dear Readers,

    Every question in this book was asked by a real kid. The kids who live in my neighborhood asked me so many questions about my dog, Fred, that I started writing their questions down. Then I decided to write the answers. I hope I've answered some of *your* questions, too.

    Sincerely,

Nancy White

Nancy White

Are Dogs Like Wolves?

NO and YES!

Dogs are not like wolves because dogs are tame, and wolves are wild. Wolves don't live in houses and eat food from a can or a bag. They live in packs with other wolves. The pack goes out hunting for food together.

BUT—even the cutest, friendliest dogs are like wolves in some very important ways. After all, the wolf is the dog's wild relative. As you read on, you'll find that dogs do a lot of the things they do because they are more like their wild relatives than you might think.

Are we really relatives?

Do Dogs Have Friends?

The answer is yes. Remember that wolves live and hunt together. And dogs are a lot like wolves. They like to have company. (Of course, every dog is different, and some are more friendly than others.)

Some dogs love to play with other dogs. Sometimes they chase each other around in circles. Sometimes they just hang out together. Sometimes they look as if they're fighting, but they're really just having fun.

Most dogs like having human friends, too. They fit into a human family the way a wolf fits into a wolf pack.

Why Do Dogs Chase Cats?

Did you ever see a can of wolf food on a supermarket shelf? Of course not, because wolves have to hunt for their own food. They have to chase other animals and catch them. (Don't think wolves are mean. They're just doing what they have to do to stay alive.)

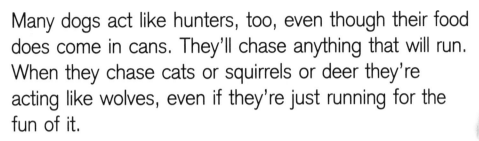

Many dogs act like hunters, too, even though their food does come in cans. They'll chase anything that will run. When they chase cats or squirrels or deer they're acting like wolves, even if they're just running for the fun of it.

Not all dogs chase cats. In fact, dogs and cats can be best friends! And some dogs who do chase cats are just doing it for fun. They wouldn't harm the cat, even if they caught it.

Why Do Dogs Bark?

In a wolf pack, barking is a signal. It means, "Danger! Watch out!" When one of the wolves in a pack barks, the wolf pups hide. The adult wolves get ready for action.

When a dog barks at home, he is usually telling his human family, "Someone's coming!"

Dogs might bark for other reasons, too—maybe they're angry, or excited. And some dogs are trained to bark when their owners say, "Speak!"

Why Do Dogs Wag Their Tails?

A wagging tail can mean different things:

"Hi! I'm glad to see you!"

"Hi! Want to play?"

or even,

"Want to fight?" if the dog's tail is held up very straight and stiff.

Does your dog wag her tail when you come home from school? That's the "glad to see you" wag.

Do Dogs Get Angry?

Some things can make a dog really angry. One of those things is another dog who wants to steal his food. The angry dog might growl. Growling means, "Leave that food alone. It's mine!" Usually, the other dog will get the message.

Some dogs get angry when strangers are around. They just don't trust people they don't know.

If a dog is really angry, the hair on his back might stand up. That makes the dog look scary. He might bark and show his teeth. That means, "See these teeth? If you don't watch out, I might use them!" (Most dogs won't bite. But if a dog is acting angry, don't even look at him. Just back away slowly.)

Are Dogs Kissing You When They Lick Your Face?

When a dog licks your face, she's acting like a wolf pup!

Dog puppies eat mushy puppy food from the store. In a wolf pack, the grown-up wolves chew up food for the pups. The pups get the mushy, chewed-up food by licking an adult wolf's mouth.

The hungry pups are so happy to get the food, that the habit of licking stays with them, even when they grow up.

So when a dog licks your face, especially around your mouth, she's saying, "Thanks for making me happy!" Isn't that a little like kissing?

When Is a Dog Grown Up?

Most dogs are as big as they will ever grow when they're just one year old! (While they won't get any taller, they might get fatter.) But they don't act really grown up until they're two or even three.

Why Do Dogs Like to Be Petted?

Puppies love to be near their mother. They're happy when their mother takes care of them. They like it when their mother licks them to keep them clean.

Petting reminds a dog of how good it felt to be licked by her mother. It makes the dog feel like a happy little puppy. No wonder dogs love it when you pet them!

Why Does a Dog Scratch Himself?

Because he has an itch!

Maybe some fleas have "camped out" on the dog's body. Or maybe it's just a plain old itch, like everyone gets sometimes.

Do Dogs Smile?

Try the experiment on this page, and see what you think.

Pat a dog gently on the tummy or give her a good scratching behind the ears. She will probably pull back her lips. Her mouth will open just a little, but her teeth will not show much.

Now try smiling at yourself in the mirror. Is your smile so different from a dog's?

Do Dogs Cry?

Dogs don't have tears. So if that's what you mean by crying, the answer is no. But dogs can let you know when they're feeling unhappy or sick. Their tails go down instead of up. They hang their heads down, too. And sometimes they make little whining, whimpering noises. That's how dogs cry.

When they feel better, they act happy again.

DR. GREY
VETERINARY

Why Do Dogs Pant?

When you run around on a hot day, you sweat. Sweating cools off your body by keeping it wet. (It's not as much fun as jumping into a swimming pool, but it works the same way.)

Dogs get hot, too. But the only parts of a dog's body that can sweat are his nose and the bottoms of his feet! When a dog pants, he breathes in a lot of cool air over his wet tongue. That helps to make the dog feel cooler.

Why Do Dogs Like to Dig?

Sometimes the wolves in a pack have more food than they can eat right away. They dig a hole in the ground and bury it, so other animals won't take their leftovers. When your dog buries something, he's hiding it away. He might dig it up someday, or he might forget all about it.

Dogs also dig for another reason. On a hot day, the ground is very warm. But the soil underneath the ground is cooler. Dogs dig up the soil to make a nice cool spot to lie down in when the weather's hot.

Sit...come...stay....

Do Dogs Understand What People Say to Them?

Most dogs can learn to understand a few words, like "sit," "come," and "stay." Some dogs get to know the names of people in their families. And almost every dog knows her own name.

But they don't understand words the way people do. So don't bother telling your dog a joke. She won't get it!

Dogs don't know many words, but they can tell if you're happy, angry, or excited by the sound of your voice when you talk to them.

Why Can't Dogs Talk?

You can talk because you have a special brain. And your mouth can make special sounds that come out as words. A dog's brain isn't made for learning words. And a dog's mouth isn't made for talking. So dogs won't ever learn to talk. (But they can tell you a lot by the way they act.)

Dogs make great friends.

But when it comes to conversation, forget it!

Why Do Puppies Chew Things?

Chewing is part of puppy play. After all, how is a little puppy supposed to know that the sock you left on the floor isn't a toy? Puppies especially like chewing on something they can shake, such as a sock . . . or something that moves, like a roll of toilet paper—things that seem to "play back."

Puppies also chew when they're getting teeth. Human babies like to chew on things when they're getting teeth, too.

Or a puppy might just think that whatever you leave around the house is something to eat. It's not so great when it turns out to be your new sneakers!

Lucky for you, most dogs stop chewing things when they grow up.

Why Are Puppies So Curious About Everything?

Because they have so much to learn! The more they snoop around, the more they find out. And the more they know, the better off they are—just like you.

Why Do Some Dogs Like to Play Fetch?

Some dogs just love it when you throw them a ball or a stick—or even a Frisbee. They'll chase it, pick it up, or catch it, and bring it back to you. This is their favorite thing to do, and they'll do it all day long—or until your arm gets tired.

Dogs who like to play fetch are really acting like wolves. Wolves chase after other animals when they hunt. Then they bring food back to the den so the wolf pups and their mothers will have food to eat. (The pups are too little to hunt. And their mothers are too busy taking care of them.)

Why Do Dogs Like People So Much?

Probably because dogs and people have been helping each other for a very long time. We know that people and dogs lived together thousands of years ago. Dogs helped people hunt. They scared strangers away by barking or even attacking. In return, people fed them and gave them a nice, safe place to live.

Dogs and people are old friends. No wonder they get along so well!

Why Are There So Many Different Kinds of Dogs?

Long ago, people figured out how to get the special kind of dog they wanted. If someone wanted a big watch dog, they chose a puppy that had big parents. The puppy would probably grow very big like his mother and father. And when that puppy grew up and had puppies of his own, *they* would probably grow big, too. But if people wanted a little dog that could sit on someone's lap, they picked a puppy with small parents.

If you want to know how your puppy will look when he grows up, look at his parents. Would you like a dog with pointy ears or floppy ears? A long tail or a short tail? What color would you like your dog to be?

Even though dogs look different, they're still all dogs! Which one would *you* choose?

Do Dogs See in Color?

Dogs *do* see in color. But the colors they see are not as bright as the colors people see.

A dog's eyes are especially good at one thing. They can see something move the tiniest bit, even if it's far away—like a little squirrel, far in the distance. Wolves notice any small animal that moves, too. Can you see how that helps them to be good hunters?

Why Do Dogs Prick Up Their Ears Sometimes?

It helps them hear better. Dogs have very good hearing. They can hear sounds from very far away. They can tell the difference between noises that sound the same to people. And they can hear sounds that are too high-pitched for people's ears.

Your dog might be able to tell the sound of your footsteps from someone else's. Or she might recognize the special sound of your parent's car from all the way down the road.

Have you ever seen someone use a dog whistle to call a dog? You can't hear the dog whistle at all, because its sound is too high-pitched for people's ears—but the dog can hear it just fine.

If a Dog Gets Lost, Can She Find Her Way Home?

How do you find your way home? You use your eyes, of course. So do dogs, but a dog uses her nose even more than her eyes!

Dogs have great noses. They can smell things that our noses could never smell in a million years, like the smell their own paws leave on the ground. So most dogs can find their way home by following their own trail of smells.

Some people tell stories about dogs who have found their way home over amazingly long distances, even when there was no trail of smells to follow! Nobody knows for sure how this happens.

Home Sweet Home

A Very Special Dog

Meet Toys. Toys is a five-year-old golden retriever. She belongs to Nathaniel. She loves to go for walks, chase a ball, and play, just like most other dogs. But she does some very special things, too.

Nathaniel gets around in a wheelchair. If Nathaniel drops a pencil or a book while he's doing his homework, Toys picks it up in her mouth and gives it back to him. If Nathaniel wants a snack, Toys can open the refrigerator door. She's still working on finding Nathaniel's shoes when he can't remember where he left them.

Nathaniel and his parents got Toys from Canine Companions for Independence in Santa Rosa, California. Nathaniel stayed at a training center in Farmingdale, New York, for five days, learning how to work with Toys. On the fifth day, there was a party, and Toys got an official diploma saying that she was Nathaniel's *assistance dog*.

Now Toys goes lots of places with Nathaniel, even places where the sign says NO DOGS. Toys has visited the Museum of Natural History and the Metropolitan Museum of Art in New York City. She has been to restaurants and traveled in airplanes, where she gets to sit in the cabin with Nathaniel.

Some of the commands Toys knows how to obey are "sit," "roll," "look," "get it," "hold," "here," "give," and "go to Mom." For the picture on this page, Nathaniel gave Toys two commands: "my lap," and "snuggle."